CW00686778

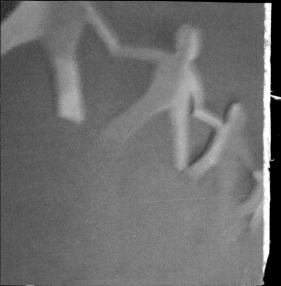

With Love to:

....

From:

....

The Gift of FAMILY
©Scandinavia Publishing House
Drejervej 15,3 DK-Copenhagen NV
Denmark
Tel. +45-3531 0330
www.scanpublishing.dk
info@scanpublishing.dk

Scripture Selection by Carol A. Kauffman
Designed by Ben Alex

ISBN 978-87-7247-292-8

THE GIFT OF
FAMILY
QUOTES FROM THE HOLY BIBLE

scandinavia

Ascribe to the Lord,
O families of the peoples,
Ascribe to the Lord
glory and strength.

PSALM 96:7 (NASB)

In the fear of the Lord
there is strong confidence,
and his children will
have refuge.

PROVERBS 14:26 (NASB)

For this reason
I bow my knees
before the Father,
from whom every family
on earth derives its name.

EPHESIANS 3:14-15 (NASB)

Every generation
of those who serve you
will live in your presence.

PSALM 102:28 (CEV)

The LORD
will love you and bless you
by giving you many children
and plenty of food,
wine and olive oil.

Deuteronomy 7:13a (CEV)

There also
you and your households
shall eat before the Lord your
God, and rejoice in all
your undertakings
in which the Lord your God
has blessed you.

DEUTERONOMY 12:7 (NASB)

And if you
and your descendants
want to live a long time,
you must always
worship the LORD
and obey his laws.

DEUTERONOMY 6:2 (CEV)

The Lord will
remember his promise,
and he will keep
the agreement he made with
your ancestors.

DEUTERONOMY 4:31b (CEV)

Yet the Lord
loved your ancestors
and wanted them
to belong to him.

DEUTERONOMY 10:15a (CEV)

He executes justice
for the orphan and the widow,
and shows His love for
the alien by giving him
food and clothing.

Deuteronomy 10:18 (NASB)

He will lead
children and parents
to love each other more,
so that when I come,
I won't bring doom
to the land.

MALACHI 4:6 (CEV)

But Christ was faithful
as a Son over His house —
whose house we are.

HEBREWS 3:6 (NASB)

Let Your work

appear to Your servants

And Your majesty to

their children.

PSALM 90:16 (NASB)

Lord, You have been
our dwelling place
in all generations.

PSALM 90:1 (NASB)

I have written
to you, children,
because you know
the Father.

1 JOHN 2:13B (NASB)

I have no
greater joy than this,
to hear of my children
walking in the truth.

3 JOHN 4 (NASB)

I also remember
the genuine faith
of your mother Eunice.
Your grandmother Lois
had the same sort of faith,
and I am sure that you
have it as well.

2 TIMOTHY 1:5 (CEV)

That the generation
to come might know, even
the children yet to be born,
that they may arise and
tell them to their children,
that they should put
their confidence in God.

PSALM 78:6.7A (NASB)

So therefore,
do not be afraid;
I will provide for you
and your little ones.

GENESIS 50:21A (NASB)

All your sons will
be taught of the Lord;
and the well-being of
your sons will be great.

For I will contend
with the one who
contends with you,
and I will save your sons.

ISAIAH 49:25B (NASB)

Their work
won't be wasted,
and their children
won't die of
dreadful diseases.
I will bless their children
and their grandchildren.

ISAIAH 65:23 (CEV)

Your descendants
will be known
in every nation.
All who see them
will realize that they
have been blessed
by me, the Lord.

ISAIAH 61:9 (CEV)

May he also be to you
a restorer of life
and a sustainer of
your old age.

RUTH 4:15A (NASB)

Your descendants
will be known
in every nation.
All who see them
will realize that they
have been blessed
by me, the Lord.

ISAIAH 61:9 (CEV)

May the Lord grant
that you may find rest,
each in the house
of her husband.

RUTH 1:9 (NASB)

For where you go,
I will go, and where you
lodge, I will lodge.
Your people shall be
my people, and
your God, my God.

RUTH 1:16B (NASB)

May he also be to you
a restorer of life
and a sustainer of
your old age.

RUTH 4:15A (NASB)

May the Lord
make the woman who is
coming into your home
like Rachel and Leah,
both of whom built the
house of Israel.

RUTH 4:11A (NASB)

Then the Lord God said,

"It is not good for

the man to be alone;

I will make a helper

suitable for him."

GENESIS 2:18 (NASB)

"Don't be afraid
of your enemies!
The Lord is great
and fearsome.
So think of him and fight
for your relatives and
children, your wives,
and your homes!"

NEHEMIAH 4:14 (CEV)

I will bless you and
give you such a large family,
that someday your descendants
will be more numerous
than the stars in the sky
or the grains of sand
along the beach.

GENESIS 22:17A (CEV)

But you, our Lord,
chose the people of
Israel to be your own,
and with your mighty power
you rescued them
from Egypt.

DEUTERONOMY 9:29 (CEV)

Honor your father
and your mother,
that your days may
be prolonged in the land
which the Lord your God
gives you.

EXODUS 20:12 (NASB)

So I will establish
his descendants forever
and his throne as
the days of heaven.

PSALM 89:29 (NASB)

When you are
suffering and in need,
he will come to your rescue,
and your families will grow
as fast as a herd of sheep.

PSALM 107:41 (CEV)

Unless the Lord
builds the house,
they labor in vain
who build it.

PSALM 127:1 (NASB)

Behold, children
are a gift of the Lord;
the fruit of the womb
is a reward.

PSALM 127:3 (NASB)

Our God,
from your sacred home
you take care of orphans
and protect widows.
You find families
for those who are lonely.

PSALM 68:5-6A (CEV)

Like arrows in
the hand of a warrior,
so are the children
of one's youth.
How blessed is the man
whose quiver is
full of them.

PSALM 127:4-5 (NASB)

Your wife will be
as fruitful as a grapevine,
and just as an olive tree
is rich with olives,
your home will be rich
with healthy children.

PSALM 128:3 (CEV)

May you live long
enough to see your
grandchildren.

PSALM 128:6 (CEV)

But I have learned
to feel safe and satisfied,
just like a young child
on its mother's lap.

PSALM 131:2 (CEV)

For you formed
my inward parts;
you wove me in
my mother's womb.

PSALM 139:13 (NASB)

May the Lord
give you increase,
You and
your children.

PSALM 115:14 (NASB)

He makes
the barren woman
abide in the house as a
joyful mother of children.
Praise the Lord!

PSALM 113:9 (NASB)

The lines
have fallen to me
in pleasant places;
indeed, my heritage
is beautiful to me.

PSALM 16:6 (NASB)

All the families
of the nations will worship
before You.

PSALM 22:27B (NASB)

I will pour out My Spirit
on your offspring
and My blessing
on your descendants;

ISAIAH 44:3B (NASB)

Grandchildren
are the crown of old men,
and the glory of sons
is their fathers.

PROVERBS 17:6 (NASB)

Teach your children
right from wrong,
and when they are grown
they will still do right.

PROVERBS 22:6 (CEV)

Even if my father
and mother
should desert me,
you will take care of me.

Psalm 27:10 (CEV)

Hear, my son,
your father's instruction,
and do not forsake
your mother's teaching.

PROVERBS 1:8 (NASB)

The Lord is always kind
to those who worship him,
and he keeps his promises
to their descendants.

PSALM 103:17 (CEV)

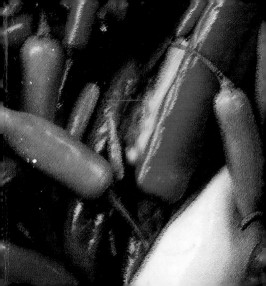

THE GIFT OF
FAMILY

THE GIFT OF
GRACE

THE GIFT OF
LOVE

THE GIFT OF
PRAYER